George Kalamaras

Through the Silk-Heavy Rains

SV

SurVision Books

First published in 2021 by
SurVision Books
Dublin, Ireland
www.survisionmagazine.com

Cover image: *Dark Celebration,* a painting
by Alvaro Cardona-Hine, reproduced with the kind
permission of Barbara McCauley (of the former
Cardona-Hine Gallery)

Design © SurVision Books, 2021

ISBN: 978-1-912963-28-7

for Mary Ann and Bootsie

and for all the plants and animals that populate these pages—

as we breathe unto them, with them, and through

Also by George Kalamaras

POETRY BOOKS

Marsupial Mouth Movements (2021)
We Slept the Animal: Letters from the American West (2021)
Luminous in the Owl's Rib (2019)
That Moment of Wept (2018)
The Hermit's Way of Being Human (2015)
Kingdom of Throat-Stuck Luck (2011)
The Recumbent Galaxy (2010) (with Alvaro Cardona-Hine)
Gold Carp Jack Fruit Mirrors (2008)
Even the Java Sparrows Call Your Hair (2004)
Borders My Bent Toward (2003)
The Theory and Function of Mangoes (2000)

POETRY CHAPBOOKS

The Shoes of the Fisherman's Wife Are Some Jive-Ass Slippers (2021)
The Mining Camps of the Mouth (2012)
Symposium on the Body's Left Side (2011)
Your Own Ox-Head Mask as Proof (2010)
The Scathering Sound (2009)
Something Beautiful Is Always Wearing the Trees (2009)
(with paintings by Alvaro Cardona-Hine)
Beneath the Breath (1988)
Heart Without End (1986)

CRITICAL STUDY

*Reclaiming the Tacit Dimension: Symbolic Form
in the Rhetoric of Silence* (1994)

Acknowledgments

I want to thank the editors of the following magazines in which all of these poems, or their previous versions, first appeared:

The Bitter Oleander: "Another Idea," "The Book of Blurred Bone," "Child-Stain Rain," "Don't Ask Me to Swallow the Japanese Scroll," "Harsh Hair," "6,000 Beards of Athos," "Unto Itself," and "When I Get Like This"

Calibanonline: "The Belt of Equatorial Calms," "The Burning, If Not Elegant Then Exact," "But You Thought Differently," "A Certain Strain of Rain," "I Don't Know How to Tell You," "I'd Be Put in a Horse," "If You Examine This Membrane," "In You," "More Monk Than Mouth," "Respectable Paragraph (On Making Love to a Literary Preface)," "Six Thousand Gold Pieces Buy the Lingering Death," "The Sorrow of Listening," "Tell Me the Buddha-Fields," "They Cannot Contain Their Sorrow," "This Roundness of Now," "You Held of Me and Coaxed the Starlings Back Through the Silk-Heavy Rains," and "You Say I Fancy the Empty Drift"

Clade Song: "Multiple Layers of the Body"

Court Green: "Lending You Your Scent"

Dispatches from the Poetry Wars: "With These Words" (in a special online anthology, *Poetics for the More-Than-Human World*, an anthology also appearing in print from Dispatches Editions)

Pemmican: "Tsunami"

Sulfur Surrealist Jungle: "Apparently Not," "Clarity," "Commands to Genii," "Every Word You Fail," "The Fourth Way In," "Great Bread," "Hidden Dialogue," "It Was Weird," "Mammal Trap," "Moons Ruining Our Mouths," "My Reputation (Into Which I Am Mapped)," "The Nearest and the Dearest," "Not to Dissolve *but* to Dissolve," "Partial Blockage of the Moon," "Unspecified Birth," and "We Stood Like Unfinished Kisses"

SurVision: "Branches of the Moon Drop Everything Small Through Me," "The Distance Between the Coccyx and the Sacral," and "The Space Inside Rain"

Talisman: "All I Have Ever Wanted," "Body Rites," "The Cutting Mouth," "Dance Lesson," "A Formula for Mirrors," "The News," "Prefect Pai Talks and Laughs and Rights a Strange Injustice," "Refusing the Bruise," "Reincarnation from the Killing Field," "Term," "There Will Always Be Generous Weather Inside the Body's Mood," "Those Lives as a Hesychast," "Unfinished Sutra with a Dozen Different Titles," "When You Imitate the Surface of Saturn," and "Why I Never Cross My Legs at a Funeral"

Word for/Word: "As We Work Our Words" and "Impossible Potato"

Great thanks to my wife, Mary Ann Cain, for decades of love and support. I also want to thank John Bradley for being my best reader, and I offer much gratitude to several friends for their ongoing inspiration and support, especially Eric Baus, Dan Gerber, Ray Gonzalez, Patrick Lawler, John Olson, Paul B. Roth, Lawrence R. Smith, and Lisa and John Zimmerman.

CONTENTS

The Anguish of Repair

On Making Love to a Literary Preface

Generous Weather Inside the Body's Mood

Elegant Glue of the Fourteenth Rib

Invigorating Starlight from Mud

The woods have stored the rain, and slow comes the smoke
  —Wang Wei

How simple and strange everything is.
  —Robert Desnos

The Anguish of Repair

They Cannot Contain Their Sorrow

So the mahogany scrape of a bleeding seed laid itself onto the
   floorboards.
So they came and plucked the shaving brush bristles, evoking the
   entire broadening of the dead wild boar.

All my internal organs rise up like Bolsheviks.
They cannot contain their sorrow at having carried me so long, so far
   from what I hoped one day to become.

Or is it joy we feel when we kiss goodbye, knowing the stars may or
   may not camp in our separate mouths?
I have sent myself off on many expeditions and always find a shaded
   fort and clear well water when I arrive.

The dead rooster was placed before me like still-quivering rhubarb.
I thanked the Huns who brought it but confided that I could not slit the
   neck.

They looked at me as if clothed in freckles.
They said something about *spotted bedragglement* and *paintbrush
   soup* and *reducing inflammation in the leopard's waul*. And took the
   neck in their large hand, revealing the scars of Eurasia.

This Roundness of Now

Then it was musk in the noise of my mouth.
I had swollen so many wounds unto myself.

I might speak the sudden wind chime of a bee.
I might resolve myself in circles of could and maybe and won't.

When the body is bitten into birth by the fire ants of Namibia.
When griffon vultures descend upon what needs to be ever more
    cleanly broken.

If you ask me my name in one of the three lost languages of salt, I
    might say, *Here, this roundness of now.*
If you deceptive and quarrel and shift.

Please, take the most tender parts of my words into you and feel the
    heron content of your blood expand with the ebullient grief of my
    most human.
Look me in the eye, with *all* of your mouths. Cry out into the leaves.
    Bring the wingèd bleed of the sycamores from you into me.

Branches of the Moon Drop Everything Small Through Me

Of the surviving copies of the original paintings, we know little.
The quality of body fragments is enough to facilitate our
    understanding—carbon dating of the bones, drawn and imagined.

Branches of the moon drop everything small through me.
He, who somehow entered the scroll without our knowing, was
    collecting dust particles with horsehair brush, beating the carpets
    apart in pursuit of lice and mites.

Who gave me three dead chickens, dealt a flexible fleece, the blow of
    botany through the sensible sieve?
Who asked whether this mouth, this time around, might actually be
    enough?

If I refuse to carry the emotional weight of others, will they leave me
    sinking into a long loneliness?
Or will it be spontaneous hurt—the way one cuts a second heart of
    apple into an oak in response to the callings of our mouths?

I don't care if I am permitted or verbally less-fractured, drawn minutely
    into a Chinese landscape among the overwhelming abundant
    simplicity of pines.
I have no use for either-or's, only for the sound of skin uncertain how
    to repair itself but finding body fragments in drops of moon
    branching out into everything.

Partial Blockage of the Moon

The debris of satellites is an intimation of perpetual motion.
You know it, like you recognize coffee plants firing foothills in Kenya.

Something is warm, as I drag myself from porridge-privilege to
    porridge-privilege.
A vanishing treasure can be as loud as an evening cemetery. We are *all*
    on our knees tonguing the lost necklace of seed sounds, whether
    we admit it or not.

The Garland of Letters, Sir John Woodroffe called it from his studies in
    West Bengal?
Tantric possibility is always present, even in the words we humble unto
    ourselves?

Purchase the green hope of a river with a concept of perfect
    articulation.
I can see the way you shampooed today, as if you planned a long life.

In the dream, three elephants gave birth to three elephants, which
    each, in turn, dispersed into nine mounds of salt.
I'd interpret it but have realized it was not a dream at all.

You'd like to know if my cable-knit sweater is hand- or machine-sewn?
You request borax in the ear as the only way to dispel the shame of
    having awakened outside your own life?

Debris in the blood is a sad depth of dirt.
Far-off stars, light-years away, die in the Tantric rivers of the left wrist.

Try what you must, but remember to respect the overleaf of a burning eclipse.

Partial blockage of the moon may dominate unseen sleep in the salt flats of the heart. Like the ache of grace lending itself for solace without sweetness or release.

Unspecified Birth

What do we celebrate when we contuse the day we were born?
An infusion of starlight in my left cheek is more manic than moist.

I am impacted to a consonant impacted to a vowel.
I no longer accept the fish history of the wrist.

I'll arrow-slip your ear with cricket-gripped might.
Soothe the heart of the hound with the exact scent of what grass floats
away in the brook.

You bought me a book about eels?
We spoke of a steady stream of bees as ontological dispersion?

Come, let me safe my breathing. Let me vault. Let me history-click my
teeth.
The terror of public *everything* corrupts my solitude with a loathsome
gas.

Afterwards, like a pagan stretch, all the angles go soft.
The hurt in the freight memory of my ear is a fractured drowse of
sound.

I went to the bookstore on my birthday and found absolutely nothing.
I remembered you going there with me, just weeks before. Leaning
toward me. Reading to me—reading *me*—not from your poems but
from a German Bible, giving me the full loud clout of a noun.

I'd Be Put in a Horse

Listen to my show of colons.
Stop : look : don't speak :

I've stalked with a limp as long as I could breathe.
Examine the photo of me at a year and a half, the cowlick suddenly
    there as if my insides were struggling with the glue of growing up.

I'd be put in a horse. I might language-lean my most Greek and dearest
    spear.
No, I am not part fish, and my name is not *Helen*—at least not on *this*
    shore.

If you start the night blessed with a parakeet, you should clean the
    dead possum of its drench of road salt.
If you analyze the process of splitting an atom, let me know the shape
    of your seizure.

With which acrobatic gasp would you like to fall from my breath to the
    galaxy?
I am skilled with aconite—monkshood—and can accommodate the
    fierce of most any beak.

Something was tearing me apart, down there below my own tricky
    ribs.
Who was hiding, and who would emerge when I most sleep?

I once trusted a semicolon to hold the entire weight of the whirl.
It held half the fires of the night; the other half was shored up by a
    horse—wooden, perfect, immobile—staring there in the protected
    space of the city of myself I thought I could never seize.

The Sorrow of Listening

This breath that keeps my breath is a living swell.
Music, maps, and motivations have guided me back life upon life.

The month before my birthday each year is an obstinate weed.
I must not have wanted to return this time to this unsure ground.

I think of a beautiful evening of almost-solid air.
The sorrow of listening to a box of cigars in their wrappers exacts a stiff
    reply.

What might we say, and how might we sway it through our mouths?
I hear distant drumming as if email does not exist.

The photograph of the beehive actually smelled of honey.
Go to your life, I heard. *Comb the labyrinth. Scratch its beard of
    intoxicating sea lice. See what wanton waters you can most willfully
    waste.*

Apparently Not

I asked a friend last week whether every kid grows up with the lance of
    an enduring sad.
Apparently not.

The emptiness in a boy's line of life can be unbearable.
Divorce at age three seems such a small thing.

Even the Queen Mother laments parting from her spider.
She places rice grains on the pillow each afternoon when she returns.

Joseph Cornell found himself face down in the hairy tail of a rabbit trap.
Meret Oppenheim, of course, was both the cup *and* the fur.

If the trail of an oxcart emits quiet rose petals, whose mouth do you kiss
    when you say, *I do*?
Why do they cheer *and* weep at the ritual touching of tongues?

I decided to buy a hotel and hire three women to sit in the lobby and
    knit.
So many patrons came just to ring the bell.

When I Get Like This

When I get like this, no one around me can wear a turtleneck.
I am not talking of my memory of trying to hide the love bite of the
    moon.

The Taoist Immortals rode their horses and fishes in on a wave.
I have tended that shore as a thin membrane of cosmically drenched
    sound.

I never wanted it to be this way.
I only expected that you'd rub red pepper flakes into my bleeding ear,
    whispering sweet raccoon names, the nocturnal scrapings of a
    polecat.

When you arrived carrying three bags of Bengali sea salt, I wondered
    why they were not folded and collapsed.
You said something about the vigor of our internal organs and the
    percentage of our bodies that is water.

I am composed and careful. I am too careful for my brain.
I will wear braids and collect the dust scars of how we grow in touching
    one another's daring below the loving wet of yet another drenched
    and drowning moon.

The Cutting Mouth

It had little to do, that life, with predicting camel races in the primitive
village outside Suhmata.
Drivers were missing due to a mangling of sand. And I was thirsty.

I handed you a piece of clay, molded into a perfect resemblance of a
Surrealist geologist.
You said *rock schist*, followed by *expensive blasting attack*, then *Robert
Desnos and the Period of Hypnotic Sleeps*.

Please, if you insist on speaking in code, return my arm hair so I might
reassemble the translation.
Feel the prolonged, inadequate, physically draining, extraordinarily
exclusive yet tiring nature of a string of useless modifiers.

The cutting mouth was given us so we could finally make things right,
living off the scythe-wise land.
We might edit our speak, slant our throat, and somehow survive.

The weight of words in the belly is spiritual leverage against the desert
heat?
A leveling of gastric juices as if we continued a working class way of
strife?

Conditions could improve if you handed me a pneumatic chisel and a
blotch of terribly compressed air.
Enter the dream. Reinvigorate the Sleeps. We often need a medium for
understanding the mysteries of the world.

My Reputation (Into Which I Am Mapped)

I wish I wasn't afraid of washing the salt, of a crack in a porcelain cup.
The tea sommelier examined my hair, as if she knew I grew up fearing
the forest green beards of trees.

Cut by a star, my chest exudes the milk of crushed bees, an offering
only moths would insist.
I was born to nourish the smallest death agonies of ants.

Delia loved trees, but it was José who got down on all fours to howl at
the moon.
I decided someone needed to piss on the grave of a poet. *Any* poet.
But one I loved. Lorca. Vallejo. Aleixandre. I drank three cupfuls of
ash from the sunburnt bodies of butterflies and joined their
exploits.

You're confused? Who, after all, is this *their*? Is it Delia? Federico? A
centipede sipping a solution of sucrose and smallpox?
You say I mix megaphones too loudly? That you can barely sear your
eye into a roast of Argentinean goat meat?

That I was supposed to be writing the lost forest poem—bamboo
splinters in the wrist, staph infections of eels growing volubly more
visible?
Honestly. Please. Give it some jest.

This discovery into which I am mapped might be called more river than
rib. More mouth than poem.
Clearly polemical, diphthongian, replete with foreign sources, I am
absent if not alive.

I brought the vulture blankets but forgot to wring them free of sand
 fleas.
I collapsed one lung just to see if I could breathe with greater ease.

Child-Stain Rain

Then there was the story of the wandering sadhu who somehow had a
   peacock tail for a lung.
He'd breathe sideways through rain and foreshadow every feathery
   snow.

Because the word *because* contains two syllables, the ginkgo refuses to
   trust the roundness of the camel's hump.
More than moonlight inhabits the Bactrian fur woven into the sweater
   draped over the living room lamp.

Nothing is connected to anything else when the word *connected* is
   used.
It's like mending the milk of a mirror. Scenting the trail of three rivers
   merging into one.

You ask about the nature of my pain, whether it is contagious simply
   by washing your feet?
You wonder whether leaving the rain and becoming human this time
   has caused me to slouch. Has left me with a slight lungfish for a
   heart.

Then there was the tale of the man who somehow had a boy
   permanently sewn into his chest.
He'd breathe sideways through rain, foreshadow every shadow he
   hoped one day to forget.

Refusing the Bruise

Can anyone speak the kava root before a leisurely fire of twigs and
  burning snow?
I was born that time as a single charred ember.

I had been a short life.
I had been an intimate breath scalding the sherpa's lung as he stroked a
  cigarette toward the pink bled of yet another Himalayan dawn.

Little dark scar I might kick away sharp.
There are no *ly* adverbs when all adjectives refuse the bruise of naming
  only by color-thrust.

Fifty million years passed before the influx of modern fish through the
  impossible ocean of the heart.
Whether we believe it or not, whether we monk-mouth or hen-eel or
  bit, we certainly *do* believe.

My speech in many ways had become hesitant. Pockmarked with
  relative success.
Anything passive might be construed as voicings of oceanic strain.

Little downpour of my heart. Can anyone speak a short life? A barely
  this, a somehow *that*? A brief bout? An evolutionary fast?
Let me taste the broken pact, the spoken act of a god.

On Making Love to a Literary Preface

Respectable Paragraph (On Making Love to a Literary Preface)

Our practice brings us to this: a man's literary twist is evidence of an
   unused world.
No Northern Song Dynasty music could find ceremonial code in such
   extreme shamanism.

Shame the shave of her leg.
Shame the salve shed from the soliloquy of my mouth in need of her
   fiercing.

I have watched of it and poured myself massive out into the starling-
   filled rain.
Hair by hair, I have smoothed-for, and oh-myed, and said my please-
   please-place-me-next-to-your-mouth.

Something is always rewriting itself in secret hair.
In the finger trace of a leg, there is an unwoven skein of private
   remorse.

After all, a moralistic preface is really quite tactical.
Literary history is to be shot, not eaten.

Don't Ask Me to Swallow the Japanese Scroll

Help me to practice that kind of compassion with myself.
It's as if every sly stance was bearing thunder.

Don't ask me to swallow the Japanese scroll.
I would never eat venison, nor the inkblot fawn, even in the name of
   art.

Everything gets resolved in the parchment star's hissing cinder.
I am here to confide that an unshaven hymn collects the fortune-
   teller's blood.

Wrap me in scarves. Sit me, calm, at the round of a watery table.
Tell me my name is *Yuri* or *Dmitri*. Even *Transylvanian Salt*.

We have come a long way through the forests and the blood.
We have squatted and lingered over the open hole, bear-sniffing our
   loss, hoping for the best.

When the full Kyoto moon entered my throat, I collected many
   shadows, many scrimmings of carp.
Now everything below the surface of the waves feels darker and more
   brilliantly lit with the fin-flash of a sinking, yet persistent,
   articulation of the moon's slow glow.

Clarity

The soothing fire of an Asian owl.
Combustible column of smoke from my chest, scouring the word *now*.

I have learned from a Great Editor that my work—though smitten with
   Eastern images—is becoming "clearer."
Do you scent the secret sutra of wind watering our mouths?

So Mary Ann and I were discussing the ironic—that tame Surrealism I've
   termed *wise-ass poetry*.
She said the most interesting thing, that the dodge around spiritual talk
   is—explicitly male or not—still gendered and largely patriarchal.

I learned from the Great Editor that my yogic lines may fall flat.
That they can be scented a mile or more off, even if I try to disguise
   them by dragging my poems through the sinks and seeps of a mud-
   chaffed river.

Then it was as if hound dogs. As if I was treed by my own secret bleed.
   As if I was iron-combed when exposing my tongue.
It was as if I had never really forgiven my own spit.

Or my spit had not forgiven me? The trembling nail nailed through my
   wrist into planks of Lebanese cedar?
The Great Editor says, *Remember this—sometimes a Christian metaphor
   is closer to "our" Western tradition and may lend greater clarity.*

The Fourth Way In

Now we come to copper in the throat.
We come to condolences. We come to regret.

We were kept busy by mounds of buckled soil.
We knew the trek would be difficult, but we undertook it anyway for
    twenty camel loads of tea.

Rapidly, I wanted to utter my own name with complete confidence.
The yogi told me days before to instead say, *Brilliant me my mouth.*

I'll confess it this way: when I came into this world, I was baptized in
    the stain of a mulberry tree.
In other words, when we entered the kitchen, it was the *kitchen* that
    was hungry.

You don't believe there were four alternatives, one of which was to
    enter India through our own way of breathing?
In the dream, someone placed a candle into my left ear and lit it with
    fossilized rainwater.

About nine miles from the oasis, I swallowed a small black stone.
No cure, no craving, no coupling to this life I had somehow grown to
    call my own.

Great Bread

Great bread troubles a collapsing ghost.
From here, it is nothing but heat and a blistered collage of copper.

I drink Tung Ting oolong tea and cleanse my bowels.
I meditate each day. I pray of and blossom a light.

Possum-eyed jingle of coins in my pocket.
The life I built on the River Wu so many centuries ago is an unknown
    Chinese ideogram standing for *the hurt-stretched skin of a swan*.

Cold lookout, as if a T'ang Dynasty watchtower could not collapse.
All along the length of insight, faint fire and a fierce form of mending.

The locust, the blacksnake, the haymow offering in which I lie.
One phrase only: *The sandwich pain of sustenance is necessary, here,*
    between equal male and female crusts.

Yes, Max Ernst's obsession with small, carved kachinas surely led to one
    of his dreams in which the sound of rain instructs a man who has
    left a horse saddened without oats.
A man with a rooster head is sticking a knife through the sole of a
    woman slung, as feed sack, over his shoulder, becoming—monthly—
    what he most wants to bleed.

It Was Weird

It was weird—my wife was understandably upset over a continual
   kitchen counter mess, as if no one in the world ate crackers as
   messy as I did.
Was her impatience anything like my causal ignorance of relegating her
   mood to Mercury Retrograde?

We each slit the pig's belly and ate the intestines thereof.
Now, what were the leeches and screw-worms trying to say through
   us?

My uncle had left the body just a few hours earlier, and I was already
   grieving.
Did the earth tilt our way a little, all the way from that breath-shift
   1193 miles north?

I remember the sound of rain in the cottonwood's throat.
I remember starlight carving the dark. Childhood woods in which I
   believed we all moved from here to there.

Our downstairs bathroom now is black *and* gold. Cleansing colors of
   carp-snap and health.
I sense balance in the way I drink and pee, pee and drink. Even when I
   imagine how others pee. How certain lovely women might
   exquisitely squat.

Which brings me to the cashew butter, crackers, and knife sprawled
   across the counter when my wife was tired and wanted a clean
   place to cook.
Sometimes I see my corpse similarly laid out, and no one is there to eat
   or clean or even grieve me.

36

I Don't Know How to Tell You

I insist that you hand me the leeches.
Don't go to church and pray for me.

Say my name isn't *Pig*.
Say it's *Recreant Recovery* or *Hand Me the Wool Shirt*.

All the dark eyes of the posters know my secret.
I'm interested in the compound fracture of a nighttime sentence.

Locate the moon-lathed wave. Find a piece of fire that seizes you.
Simple words like *yes* and *toe*, *finger* and *solar plexus*.

They have now proven that the brains of cab drivers grow in proportion
    to the strategies of streets they map.
What we take in, takes us. The sense of guilt in large cities must be
    unbearable.

Hand me the sea lice. Scent me your hair. Grant me access to the hermit
    crab in its nocturnal crate by your bedside.
Let me molt a new shell for you each night as you sleep. You will barely
    hear me scraping my body awake just a few aching feet away.

Those Lives as a Hesychast

Forgive me if I return to those lives as a Hesychast.
So much of me now has been shaped by all I could never achieve.

Variety, they say, is the hallmark of Tanzania's Game Reserves.
I cannot tell whether I prefer the double-breasted or hairy-breasted
  barbet.

In 1923, André and Clara Malraux journeyed to French Indochine in
  search of a forgotten Khmer temple.
I tell you this—it is not wise to lift a few relics and try to make a killing
  on the European market.

Nor is it spiritually sound. This is the story of a formidable brilliance.
The story of a first rumbling of war resembling an independent
  incitement in the chest.

So what does this have to do with those lives I spent as a Hesychast
  monk?
Did I fake Byzantium, the bejeweled cross on the cloth of a Mount
  Athos altar, in order to get Brahms to relinquish fire ants he'd
  implanted—with minor chords—into my left wrist?

Let's put it this way: a Megaloschemos monk wearing the Great Habit
  is more than a daily practice, more than a river resembling a
  meandering slack.
The Gombe Stream Game Reserve on the northeastern shore of Lake
  Tanganyika was established in 1945 primarily to protect the
  chimpanzee population, dwindling—it was reported—among the
  shuttle-scruff of laying their fists while walking too long in the
  waste of their brethren.

38

6,000 Beards of Athos

Because we'd camped there once for many decades as sea lice.
Because all we had were the surrounding Aegean and the perplexity of
   endomites.

Because once, when I was young, there was actual apple biting.
I wondered if I couldn't be useful as a worm, degenerate my tiny dung
   into reified excrescency.

The bullet of an assassin's story includes life—even as told by a monk?
Depth of the most exhausting voice in the world is somehow Orthodox,
   hiding whatever it can in metaphors of donkey bray and blame?

We'd been instructed never to touch the apple inside our night cells.
We'd been warned that touching it even there might reduce the primacy
   of our prayer.

So we lived among the beards *as* beards, even as the cantor shook the
   censer and assumed the lotus posture before the altar.
We plucked a goldfinch from each of our ears, claiming ourselves inane.

This is not to suggest the trembling tissue of the body was not pure.
I hid my monk mouth with mustachio and beard—my own personal nest
   for saliva, egg yolk, and the low moans of private nightly shame.

More Monk Than Mouth

Ghost-fish for walleye, and we find a conglutination of obstinacy and
   public rain.
Make the moon one or more ways of mouth.

Move monk-wise toward the entire week of June collapsed into a
   monthly kiss.
The beetle-killed pine does not remember December frost. No, I am
   not dead.

I have been snail light in the overcast day.
The time of dark and cool slowly makes my hermit self come alight.

And so we took the towels, folded them lengthwise into what would
   become water.
And so the tubs of pain were waiting for the slow, for the deliberate of
   a single word-urge.

To somehow smooth away the air bubbles given us at birth is
   equivalent to the sunflower fierce of a kiss.
My pain is that all pains swift through me, somehow craving my ache.

Drift, now, in the undercurrent seed. Go gold as any carp wasp-bitten
   and sung.
The way an African tree ant is suddenly displaced in the season of fire
   might mean blocked rain in the bloated body of a flea.

I have been handed the lantern-cast, locked—as it were—in the occult
   centers of the spine.

I come up scar-bitten, blood-gilled. Home in the time of dark and cool.
  Clearly more monk than mouth. More human than love. In the slow.
  In the slow deliberate of speech.

Impossible Potato

It was late afternoon, and I could see the village of Olosenga.
Even the island elder had stopped the eastern sky from becoming a
scarlet of rotting fish.

With a total population of twenty-three, all my ceremonial dead had
said, *Everything you've ever talked will haunt.*
I could only count the memory of each gypsy moth I had killed, the
exact wing sting, the way my mouth struggled for warmth.
Struggled to fly sideways at times when listened to but not broken.

The wingspan of a tropicbird must be some immense expanse.
For ten days at ten o'clock, a panacea of human ills presented a great
toxicity.

Had I known to expiate the exacting stance.
Had I only thought to live myself clean, dig for root vegetables inside
this hat dance or that.

So, in another life, you had twirled around more than one renegade
fire, calling yourself *Duscha* and *Anitchka.*
I died each time your skirt, my darling, hiked daringly above the crease
of your knee.

Breathe me slow or not at all in the whirling dance of your lovely
damp.
Kill me before the waning fire and wagon dust. My mystical rut, your
thigh, your full gorgeous hips. This servitude of my spiritual
stomping ground in the kerosene rag of your stamped lamp.

Moons Ruining Our Mouths

Then there was the story of the sculptures that refused to speak.
The moon had emerged, gathering a massacre of moths.

Fantastic animals populated our mouths.
They brought extreme beginnings to conversational endings.

Our retinue included pack animals and Tibetan lamas with shaved heads
    and large black umbrellas.
I even found one detachment of broken sunlight impersonating dawn.

Sure, we understood that our tongues were the only way out.
How to control our speech became a meditative act, more solemn than
    digging for snails.

When we got to the close of the book, there was a foldout map.
When we tried to open it, dust from Algeria had crossed the great
    ocean, partially dimming our view.

The sky could not talk. The trees could not talk. The animals could not
    talk.
Even the soup in our bowls at the close of the day's journey refused the
    earth's brutal bruise.

Then there was the story of fantastic moons ruining our mouths.
There were flowering peacocks and those that had been plucked, the
    latter strolling around colorless but calm, taking to higher ground to
    display both their love and fear of the unceasing agony of release.

As We Work Our Words

In those days, I was apt to read anything slantwise through my throat.
If you said, *Belgian Congo*, I might hear, *medicinal mouth present in the
photosynthesis of the cinchona tree.*

If you told me, *Kiss me, my secret darling*, I might hear, *Please remove
our tongues, two at a time.*
If you confided that you love seventeenth-century Japanese erotic art, I
might understand it as, *I adore you most when, naked on the toilet,
you resemble a painting we've never been able to quite live.*

I know. I'm at it again. Always shuffling—clumsying—the various
passages of our mouths. And how our bodies swell.
Yes, I see how perfect your imperfections and kiss you in the dark to
prove it.

Yesterday, I was jostling tumblers in a lock, reciting the scientific names
of each species of sparrow in the most northern prefecture in
Japan.
When I got to the genus, *Pull it tight*, I did not know if it meant your
hand, your agony, or the mystical bloom between our mouths.

On the surface of the sun, we all reinvent the multiple ways we might
burn our bodies anew, the eternal clockflower and Scorpio's sting
into the crab's watery deeps.
Much less involved, yet perhaps more compelling, is the fragrance of a
galaxy falling apart as we work our words to mean something—
anything—almost human, almost nearly divine.

Generous Weather Inside the Body's Mood

The Space Inside Rain

Next we take up the space inside rain.
Do you remember my previous death, the one from the floods?

The onset of blackwater fever was an optical sign.
No matter how many cables were sent, not a single peafowl could be
  saved.

What I have in my throat is a clumsy protectorate.
Someone drank my entire body, beginning with pocket lint.

The crutch collapses. I welcome you to the next world.
The African violet bends bluish-white as if there was never any music.

I become the ebullient washerwoman. I become Anushka, the Banaras
  woman at the fish market with no shoes. Mohan and the leather seat
  of his bicycle rickshaw.
It is not colonization to imagine other small deaths of the moon pouring
  kerosene into the morning sea?

I now know the name for *winter solstice*.
I am a shoemaker mending boots through the long night with Jacob
  Boehme in a lantern-lit cottage in a cobblestone village.

The space inside rain is as raw as a breakfast without lamps.
All kinds of tongues cannot depress Ganges floods from recurring.

We say our words. We stitch them just right.
We are invisible for one day, walk among the gods, sunk into our shame.

In You

Because I wore sheepskin I could detect the movement of microscopic
   mites whose entire life cycle—from emergence from the egg to
   laying their own—is only three or four days long.
Even before the exchange of starlight for blood, you could pour me
   into a glass of water and expect nothing but strength and tonal
   dissolve.

A sugar cube is not equivalent to dysentery dormant in a pinch of salt?
You respect me in the morning but refuse to baste my eggs?

Yes, the homeless are most on fire on the boulevard of my heart.
That doesn't make bathing with a damp blue rag across my chest a
   reason for insanity.

The cute cashier filed a report and blamed my ectoplasm for her haptic
   condition.
It began, *He glanced at me from across the street, and I felt lightning
   enter my spine.*

You could ulcerate my name, blame me *more or less*, even *less than or
   equal to*, and I would not complain.
You could illuminate the mark of my dark, tell me the x-ray of your arm
   hair includes the intimate now of my mouth.

This is not simply an exercise in channeling bodily heat.
Recursive discourse, I say. *The practice of an eel farm on fire. Drench of
   our dearest most direct death.*

I'll tell you what sticks. This resin in my wrist. This sap of a word. Certain
   birth sores I bore.
Otherwise, the bulk of my passing sadness resembled the autumnal
   movements of certain birds.

With These Words

And so I discovered that my body was composed of Chinese blood
    pheasants.
In panda time, dark black circles surrounded even the bloodletting with
    hope.

I came away from the mirror wishing I was thinner.
My pants pulled tight. I remembered the gaseous bloat of chickpea-
    kale soup.

In those days, I'd made the arctic fox my totem. Her milk-blanched fur.
    Even her stool.
It was a blistering Indiana January. I imagined her several weeks north
    eating the decomposed hoof of a dead musk ox.

I felt my skin flush with feathers.
I stayed inside and avoided cookies, cashews, and mirrors.

Adult hares, I knew, belong to a measure of extraordinary sparseness.
They birth their leverets, followed by an eloquent squabbling to hide
    among the frozen stones.

When disturbed, two of my hands resemble the edge of any body
    remembering the electrical charge of snow-aching rain.
Seasons within seasons. Totems within toes. These words, secretly
    composing. Composed. Of blood birds our bodies, together,
    continue to bloom.

When You Imitate the Surface of Saturn

Now we come to the emptiness inside.
We come as night-growing plants. We come as estranged gnats.

It is the same fierce itching. A similar mangy cave.
Scabies in the wrist. Pungent as lamb dung.

Whom do you fresco when you imitate the surface of Saturn?
Why have you turned me into an unrepentant verb? Why have you
   stranged and heat-sunk and shitake-mushroomed the stew?

A bowl of all kinds of tendered animal tongues willingly accepts
   cauliflower with cumin.
I have no body in my no-more throat, no any-human-pain.

Then there's the parable of the moon judging my slantwise slant.
The ribcage of the barn lifts all night with Bactrian bird wind. With a
   threat of starlings at sunrise.

I am exact if not precise. I am singular if not pineal.
Millions forget how many millions of sighs remain. Suture us clear.

Term

That, of course, is not us—only a bone suture, purchased monthly from
   our pay.
An insidious nostalgia plagues me life to life.

For what restoration might I hobble my limp?
Consider why history undergoes invention, why the molecules of
   broken Ethiopian clay pots are salvaged and reused as carriage
   house bricks in Connecticut and Tennessee.

Nor does the merciless winter cooperate.
Last night four inches of snow buried a bed of ice like a conspiring
   thug.

I might unlook a brief appeal as I descend the stair and open the door.
Who might be waiting to touch me with guilt? How did they track my
   mouth—through all these incarnations—all the long way here?

A throng of coffin floods may or may not be recognizable.
At any rate, yes, *hyphenated sleep* joined all sorts of things together
   and became more than an annual term payment. More than a
   wobbling word-phrase.

Nine months labor on a rock bed of hard ice?
No magic tact when we try to finally make things right? Emerge from
   oceanic depths, pierced by a pufferfish?

Let's settle it once and for maybe. I was born because I *needed* to be
   born.

There are so many karmic seeds to expunge, this time, in the cool fires of the brain, waiting for the egg release of eels electric with ecstasy along the altar of the spine in the moment-moist mouthings of now.

But You Thought Differently

Slaughter your resistance to any terrible thing.
Glance at a Chinese Song Dynasty impulse as if you hated history in all
its release.

Wear a star. Wear a star and inflict upon it the gauzy pulse that pulled
it down.
Inflect it this way: *Can the chipped tooth ever measure up to the
Malaysian thrush on fire in the thatched Bornean hut?*

All right. Instead, one day join the sorrow of a mynah bird.
See it for what it isn't—that you've grown beyond primitive projection.

No one gets entirely past the sad stance of their hands.
It's like drinking the staph-ridden obsession in a strangely held cup of
tea.

The master of the razor has an infinite strop.
Oil it. Take it through the eye of a needle. Watch the camel squirm.

In love's *other* way, bend at the knee and sniff.
A weeping willow brushes the earth, inhabits the lamps you thought
swayed toward you in the slow motion of underwater speech.

There Will Always Be Generous Weather Inside the Body's Mood

A marred mound of starlight does not comfort China's furthest moon.
It does not sink Upper Volta below Lower Volta—or beneath any urgent
    digging.

I used to think it was not that difficult to burrow through dirt to the
    earth's core.
Then I was born.

I lit a torch with kerosene rag in search of my own cleanly bathed egg.
The immune system of an anemone stings even the most lavish glance.

There will always be generous weather inside the body's mood.
The wind stops. The mouth cannot help but make moments in the moist.

If you died of dehydration, were found hankyless in the sand—without
    even a red bandana—might they call you, *Salt, He Ate Some Salt*?
Would they slit themselves silly, beg the moon's beached fish back the
    strange way they came?

Endless symmetrical hour of growth.
Of trimming one's own ivy back so that it won't make you bleed.

All this brings me to the shallow sound, the shark in my ribcage
    thrashing and trapped.
All this speaks, *Yes, I have a damp breath, a sound that continuously
    moves through a cataract of confused already-breathed air.*

If You Examine This Membrane

A botanized sequin pretends to be a leaf-shadow.
What if I knelt a bridge between Hindu chanting and American jazz?

Imagine Mingus with a harmonium. Swami Sivananda smoking a Lucky.
What would be the song, and how might the fire ant find a way to
   remain dead?

However, I do not combine messages with unencumbered geese salt.
If you examine this membrane, you might recall that dream of finding
   an astrological bangle embedded within the seasoned skin.

It's nothing, really, this reach for common speech.
I can't imagine another way of stalking the canebrake for what has so
   long salted me.

Heavy mistakes arrived in the wets, flopping this way and that like
   potential questions.
Each swam for centuries, did something wrong without considering the
   consequences. The karmic shits of panting again and again over the
   stool.

The Book of Blurred Bone

An ecclesiastical bone that was bent into a brook.
The essential nutrients swore it was the kale that gained them strength.

I had asked a question that did not have a reply.
I stood the woods, scratching my name from the parameter of the
number three.

Elm-bark thatch I could and I might.
Each branch in the shape of Father, Son, and Unseen Horse Chestnut
Root.

Down below, I could hear the lower chakras rumble.
I cannot describe the secret sound. It is enough for you to drink a
blustery milk of bees.

I decided we both needed a morning of whole oats.
We might once again survive in fulfilling the cinnamon purpose of a
spoon.

We lay together, in the afterbath, completely unclothed, her back to me,
receiving my most tender love.
I counted the freckles on her shoulder, my knees tucked below her
buttocks, and carefully read to her passages from *The Book of
Blurring Bone*.

Multiple Layers of the Body

Now we come to the celebration of cranes.
I once was a crane. You were a crane. We all ate fish.

Hear my cry across Poyang Lake in Jiangxi Province?
Feel the lower Yangtze basin itself into a vast migration.

Even an ordinary air burial blesses the snow.
The gliding rites of conifers and the crags of heaven pierce my bliss.

Any erratic movement—not just sipping fire from the bodies of dead
    lightning bugs—sends increased blood to the cells, to all the
    sleeping limbs, including the ghost-flock of cranes.
Stroke my black-speckled neck. Wingbeat the wind. Call me only by the
    first names that each of the lamps have—in draining their oil—
    given the delirious bloat of gnats.

Prefect Pai Talks and Laughs and Rights a Strange Injustice

Yellowing paper on the desk and six feet of gauze.
With the help of friends, we might find the inimical demands of death.

I had an enemy. She had a friend.
The weaving-shop owner passed a thread right through the heat of the
    cold.

That had been in my chest. Words attempted to climb us right, as if
    afflicted with other words.
It was like trying to build a piece of sky, one ladder foot at a time.

He sat on a tiger skin mat, closed his breath, and explored the heavens.
He tapped me here in the chest—just a glance—and I too was gone for
    one, long, infinite breath.

Someone needed grounding. Anyone.
Someone was crying out from lice bites on the tongue. With the
    affliction of a language-bitten life.

Lead the donkey down the stone path of what, in us, is mostly echo.
Walk across the way my first and only word remains my last.

Unfinished Sutra with a Dozen Different Titles

The Trouble with Being Human.
Yes, I Really Do Eat Twigs.

A History of Because.
The Catastrophics.

If in Eating an Aspirin I Were to Sway.
Why Are the Words "Real Fun" Embedded in the Word "Funeral"?

A History—of Course—of History.
Turn Off the Spectrometer (To the Tune, "Heal Me Now My Mouth").

Winter Kill Awaiting the Killing Frost Awaiting the Sweat-Stained Shirt.
The Light Goes on Lying.

The Secret Life of Indiana Voles (As Performed in Rain).
Here, Hold the Casserole for Seventeen Seconds While I Pee.

Unto Itself

I am receiving messages from long-dead fireflies, imprinted in the ether.
I have seen the folded flower, the shape of the number eight doubled
   over into an underground zero explaining the cost of a single life.

When the musical equivalent reveals conversation, it is often an echoing
   hallway.
I sought her salt-washed voice, spoken volubly like the impersonal
   shuffling of agonized shoes.

We introduced a broad mistake so as to compel a complete change of
   engagement.
Beginning with the ending, I continued to examine the sorrow of my
   many lives.

I continued to taste peacock saliva whenever I washed my face.
I recalled how I'd recalled I might actually have reassembled my own
   skin.

Did any amount of washing tell you how totally I had softened my voice?
Did a kind issue between us become love in my arms, or a history—
   emphatic and complex—unto itself?

Elegant Glue of the Fourteenth Rib

Harsh Hair

I hear your solitary mouth dwell dark inward vegetation.
You interrupt my broken scar as if measuring peculiar piercings of sleep.

How could I not destroy your harsh hair?
How could you line my cleaning rag with vats of shadowy jasmine?

My imperfect ash will soon blow away.
Everyone who attends will leave my pyre with an empty tear duct due to
  my tenacity.

I'm not sure I want any of them to remember anything specific about
  me.
I would be pleased if they'd place a stone in their mouths, contact the
  locusts, and walk off shaking their heads, muttering, *Who was he
  anyway?*

I remember an interminable oblivion, a vague territory called *Life*.
I wandered the desert, dressed in camel-hair rags, pleading your hand
  for a dowry of well water.

If you burn my gaze, interrupt my bones, my rose-branch breath might
  never break, even amidst the stench of burning hair.
I will you my symmetrical thorn. Then my words, to penetrate your sad
  with the cremation sash of animal noise flaming into something no
  longer human but beautiful.

Six Thousand Gold Pieces Buy the Lingering Death

The epigram is probably fictitious.
When cinnabar is burned, the most common way of stretching is
  probably an echo.

I am convinced that the color of attraction is a calming seafoam green.
We sniff one another like dogs in order to grasp every grass of our
  past.

There is a stereotypical expression—*Death is the end of death.*
It is not common but known in the game comprised of thirty-two
  dominoes and a shoal of paired seahorses.

A caricature of my simple labor haunted me incarnation to incarnation.
I knew I had a past, which was one reason I got down on all fours to
  defeat it once every whingeing wind.

It was ordered that I was to report to my imagination, punctually, on
  the third day of the third week of every third month.
Everywhere is an aphorism about me that has something to do with
  salt.

Let's try it together: *He agonized over the cruel cruel salt-craves of his
  heart.*
Or this: *The black piping on his pants was the linear stain of how his
  victory dream continued to bleed through.*

The epigram will certainly be fictitious.
The epitaph may say he never truly lived.

She wore a blue cotton skirt that clung flatteringly to her hips. Not even six thousand gold pieces could buy him a way out.

Mammal Trap

Yes, I lived many former lives on the banks of the Ganges.
They were not unlike dividing myself across centuries as slivers of
   smoke. As paramecia performing puja on a candlewick.

I don't care if you don't believe me.
Believe *this*—this upright scar I call a body, this fourteen-hundred-year
   bread crust, this discipline of wearing shoes.

One day you're pulsing—perfectly content—in the larvae of lice,
   embedded in the chest hair of a renunciant.
Then you're suddenly crawling on all fours, pissing your pants, begging
   your mother for milk.

This custom has persisted from the time of bones and fire. From the
   first days of the horse sacrifice.
We might find a sudden mound of stinging ginger ants. Locate
   considerable concern for filariasis, dysentery, and yaws.

Each night I'd collect kisses, tiny feathery swirls on *my* neck or hers.
I'd light a candle and tighten the wax, life after life, trying to placate
   my need.

I lived so many lives, I became not just a paramecium or renunciant's
   cloth sack or—in one rebirth—a momentary flake of considerable
   ash. Once, I even became each of seventy-three traps set out for
   small mammals.
In the teeth of the dark's dark, in the powerful jaws of this desire or
   that, I thought I could finally die. Alive.

Lending You Your Scent

Do you recall the shaved leg, your underarm scar, my prayer beads
made of apricot pits?
Do you recall the way we touched, that lifetime? And how we brought
forth the dark flower?

I have been crying *Mexican sombrero* as long as I could survive.
I have tossed the baby out with the *I Ching* coins onto the table.

The other one, the one who is *not* Vallejo's spleen.
Ask her if it is sweeter inside the dead bees of a star.

That one, the one in the wall grate, is tinier than the bone-chipped wrist.
Insure us both for maximum coverage. And then undress my sad.

If you lend me your ache, I will grant it a bath of hands.
I will add it to my collection of honey-hungry moths. Of my moments of
any-human-pain.

How many births did I recall as you opened me, opening your arms,
lending me your scent?
I will be with you, now and always, even unto the end of our sex.

The News

A kind bloodletting followed me through the kitchen.
I considered hesitant headlines and a dubious dragonfly.

How many Mormon Crickets could you kill against your bumper during
an eight-hour drive from Denver to Billings?
I elected to please my tongue with the taste of lentils, rubbed the
doorknob, and scratched a rash of morning rain?

I know. I'm at it again—questioning even my question marks?
If I went around town with an unused voice, who would suspect my
forehead of mitigated music? Of unmitigated woe?

I brought in the passport. Saw inked circles of travel. Watched the all-
night news as I sat in my memory of the 2 a.m. blizzard of a 1962 TV
screen.
I thumbed my nose at popcorn with burnt organic butter for the sake
of a pound or two less.

Whatever actually pisses us off might be a passel of bees from decades
before or a bedlam from afar.
Mouth my noun. Stay it in the dark. Tell me the news is wrong.

Tsunami

Upon any mention of a crowded color wheel, something is suffocating
   the breeding habits of saffron.
It is not like stripping the shellac of the floor. More like 154,132 days of
   unsorted mail.

When we reached early afternoon, morning was already two naps back.
Yes, we admired the train, but when the stranger told us it was due to
   the duality of the track, we relocated our weeping.

You think me silly? You consider the characteristics of emotional
   collaboration a hoax?
I challenge *you* to live even fourteen days alone with a dead parakeet
   and examine the moods ingesting *your* sad.

Your weeping, my wife had told me, *is part of the dualism.*
The poem should show what the weeping could be.

The same violent weather appeared to mirror the same violent paths we
   chose to bomb a continent away.
Wave upon wave of emotional dross, of crossbred color schemes, might
   confiscate the track.

Dogma. Dictum. Shifting oceanic plates of malarial mystical mistake.
Dichotomous mouth with which I am rail-spent and slung.

Yes, no. Right, wrong. This, that.
This is not an antiwar poem. No, wait—*yes* it is.

Reincarnation from the Killing Field

That was when I grabbed the pan of fried rice and tried to find the iron
   scalding my shirt.
It was the time of blood in the clocks. A century of sand in the wrist.

I would sometimes turn a hummingbird upside down to count each
   grain of blood.
I would pace the house as if expecting a fourth child from my fifth
   unborn daughter.

So different language tongues were comfortable and completely at
   home in my speech.
I might memorize every sentence in my memoir, *In Loving Me, They
   Feed Me Crocodile Dung: Then They Might Kill Me.*

Little strawberry light about to auburn-braid my hair. Come eel-like
   into my stance.
Activate centuries of spiritual longing. Longing for release.

So I became attentive to Kundalini. To the goddess Kali.
So, I should say, my gorgeous past gorgeously attracted exactly my
   need.

There was a pile of skulls in the killing field and a national
   spokesperson who could be reached only by unbuttoning the left
   cuff of every right-handed shirt.
When she answered, she swore she never knew me, or at least had not
   known I'd been in the vicinity all those years speaking Macedonian,
   Khmer, or Japanese.

The Burning, If Not Elegant Then Exact

The Maasai warrior who wrote an autobiography.
The color blue and its remnant of even the slinkiest green.

There is no crushed oil of apple-seed delight.
We have eaten many varieties of olives and agree on the duplicitous
    manner of the pits.

Is there a way to charge ahead and relinquish the spurring width of the
    season?
What brings my mind exact if not the quieting of already-quiet breadth?

Elegant glue of the fourteenth rib. Elegant voice of stopped attack.
I am glad of it and done and wait-till and compressed.

You express your stool as if showing a rare and exotic mirror.
I hear the voice of everything beautiful, as if the world was truly fluid.

So now Maasailand becomes another name for *Recalcitrant Mother*.
We cross a great joy, a great dry gorge, and witness the yoke of a
    clutched tongue. The sudden burning of sheep. Curds of the recurring
    herd.

Another Idea

Another idea that seemed good had something to do with nocturnal
    death.
Now and then, the finches reflected our desire for dark, dark sky.

Presently, I am mindful of that one remaining bale of hay.
The man called me baleful, but the metaphor was contrived.

The Congolese had been more than eager to trade lives.
I sought adventure and they the stability of a reliable hunting gun.

Following the lead of the wet nurse among our band, I placed my hand
    against any fullness I could.
There were orchids the size of pants, the inseam of my jeans reaching
    toward angry fish or a warm swarm of bees.

Charlie grew a beard and abandoned the boredom of mending
    mosquito nets for the duration of the night watch.
I forgot about the creepers and positioned my body in the hung slung
    of a hammock somehow swaying the way our words fell apart
    between species, between trees.

Sure, the turkey buzzards mistook me for proliferous death.
When they circled with their delighted cries I was no longer sure that—
    however many lives I had lived—I was meant to survive.

A Formula for Mirrors

And still I experienced foreign history as a year and a half in the eye of a
  fish.
No book adequately depicts the meaning of brutally nuanced war.

The openhearted dog flushed a kind bird from the sullen man's chest.
He kept an egg in a plastic box as if initiating the fluids of a cosmogonic
  mouth.

More accurately, I realized I was a sharp observation.
My remarks were overly pointed. My conversations heated. And I
  delighted in the steaming of chickpea stew and kale.

From an old melody, a few time-deathed smells.
When the honored windows mumbled into discontented mouths, we
  sought the formula for mirrors.

Still, I'd like to employ a jeweler to unpack the luminescence of a
  marsupial pouch. Fill its banditry of teeth and every pleading mouth.
That hole in the sun keeps leaking an emphatic everything.

Sure, it would be a good idea for me to finally make a mistake.
It might protect me, one day, from doing any real harm.

Commands to Genii

I'm pondering that unused title of Stevens'.
Of course, I imagine three wishes of what his poem might have been.

Sure, I have given an aspirin to the cow, so now I am no longer worthy
    of selling woodsmoke as forsythia.
You might fashion me a jackass, send me, say, to Salamanca to browse
    the lemon balm and shrubs.

I have been given a chance at a new bone.
Suture by suture, its door of impossible fear encompasses my
    sentence.

If, line by line, we write to live, what are we to do with the voles owls
    sonically hunt through night soil and strain?
If we unpack the etymology of the word *Genii*, how might our left
    shoes command the lack of hands on the right?

So much dark and blight.
So much order to the chaos in the intentionally misplaced thread of a
    Navajo weave.

Hurricane this, you say. *Moon-mouth that.*
The doctor's table marks the edge of one of many bones.

John Zimmerman, my friend the chiropractor, tell me: from where
    does your skill derive?
Hands? you ask. And I say I have felt my muscles clap back—three
    times—to some proper order when read to, melodiously, in the
    voice of any blackbird in a hurricane off the Florida Keys.

Why I Never Cross My Legs at a Funeral

The circumference of salt is a ragged outline of deranged clock hands.
We sank swiftly into the superstition of Greek grandparents and, thus,
    never laid a hat on a bed, opened an umbrella in the house, or gave
    someone a knife without selling it to him or her for a penny.

It resembles the folly of lingering smoke, as if it were a corner hoodlum.
Jingoism may or may not be intentional. Even crushed bees in the spine
    of a dead possum do not care.

If the crew devoted itself to washing the movie, more than film canisters
    would get ruined.
What about those parts of ourselves we've left in the snow-vasts of
    Zhivago's St. Petersburg? In Bogie's and Bergman's everlasting fog in
    Morocco?

European fears ranged from getting married during a leap year, to
    breaking a mirror, to dropping a fork or a knife.
Still, I never cross my legs in a church or at a funeral.

A further disturbance to rouse my Greek-blood sleep was not required.
We threw salt over the shoulder. Ate what was left. Inherited the bloat.
    And the men among us got moody on a regular basis at the passing of
    a black cat, at the opening of an umbrella in the house, or as we
    walked down a street with a ladder from the Old Country blocking
    our way.

You Held of Me and Coaxed the Starlings Back Through the Silk-Heavy Rains

I am not afraid of your words. I am constituted of your hips.
I am a piece of torn sheet. A speck of oolong tea. I am breadcrumbs
    not yet dead.

For a long time, the clarity of touch replaced me, starling by starling.
I recognized my past, filled with jars of sugar and granules of spoiled
    milk.

Each of our internal organs recognizes the other.
No, we have not previously met, but I am certain to be your psoriasis.

I had been born, once, in Chiba Prefecture—among silk-heavy rains—
    resisting yet another birth.
You held of me and coaxed, your thigh-tight and full-breasted wanton
    of my lip.

Burying an airmail stamp in a wooden box in the backyard seems
    obsolete.
I have held the porcelain flight, the imagined texture of rain.

This summer, come to me. Come *through* me. Open your blouse. Soil
    our mouths without any fixed sense of flesh.
Come through all the torn stars of the Milky Way. Don't *ever* let me
    stray from my life. Promise me the possibility of your impossible
    perfection.

Invigorating Starlight from Mud

Hidden Dialogue

And so I come to fear and how I am completely done with it.
We come to condolences. We cross our mouths out with soap.

What precisely *was* a yellow wasp, and how many other meanings did
    kibachi have in Japanese?
I found dead skin on the bed sheet and recognized the onset of a new
    day.

Besides uprooting the dialogue hidden in a vocal cord, I was at a loss.
Words reminded me of a card game played over the dead body of a flea.

What are you holding when you look at me through the eel shiver in
    your cheek?
How many bee entrails are smeared, glowingly, on the inside of our
    body caves?

We finally see something beautiful after many confused lives.
We had once been hyenas exchanging saliva on the cruel salt flats of our
    brains.

All I Have Ever Wanted

Now we come to the study of salt-blood.
The way a crane stalks the canebrake, flies through the mudflats of the
    body's cells.

A farmer from Kansas mows a mumbly sheep.
A rancher in Montana curses burnt rows of corn.

Everything is switched achingly around.
Ancient buffalo bones belong to my mouth, the polished remains of an
    extinct instinct.

All right, you bastards, you think me sane?
Crazy how I rip apart a precise excavation of language to reveal
    oxblood soup in the steaming sockets of your mouth?

Now we come and study and salt-blood the books.
We how and why and salt-maybe our mouths.

We ranch-fast the sheep back to the corrals of corn.
We ancient and polish and dismember our remembering of the
    remains.

The way a whooping crane flies through the fish. Culls the swampy
    dark.
The way these words, the exoskeleton of all I have ever wanted to eat.

Dance Lesson

I couldn't redeem my bellflower but took the ash of a possum's eyelash
    as a source of strength.
No one quite knew why I sang in avalanche. In a voice of many snows.

The immensity of an ice field as an exact explanation of my past
    thoroughly excuses the casualties as consent.
To give both spare sofa cushions away, as my wife suggests, may seem
    sensible, but is it a redeemable situation?

I thought about blood. I considered an engorged human ear.
I imagined myself as Van Gogh donating my buttons to the poor.

They say a list of typhus cures may prove inconclusive, that we are shot
    through with our past in ways only the malarial mouths of
    mosquitoes may know.
Everyone thinks of the poor, especially when they bow to the evening
    cauliflower on the cutting board and admit a certain loneliness,
    confiding, *Please, don't let me be eaten first.*

I overcame the sadness of your hair, though mostly during the unknown
    holidays absorbed through the furnace grate.
I wore a coat I couldn't close, sat on an old worn couch, and watched
    distant films of how I'd earlier thought things *would* be, counting the
    elegant steps of Fred Astaire and Leslie Caron.

Tell Me the Buddha-Fields

Are you shawling the sky, the northern-most wind of Montana?
Are you shouldering even the faintest pink of a sunburn you imagined
from the underbelly of a mole?

I was a seed of liquid wind. Warm. Star-bitten.
Something kept planting me in hard ground, imparting desire and a
unique name each time I was born, then leaving me with the
raccoons to scour the midnight cribs of corn.

Patterns of blood awaken the love of austerity.
I remember other lives, mole-driven, when I lived in a monk cell with
nothing but a candle, a sound carving knife, and a cake of soap.

Any minute now, you could be the hen-eel forming my blood.
When the sacred spinal serpent stirs, all the body cells awaken.

Shake out the coriander seeds from your hair.
Make music with the wind's moist. Your body's terrible blue bridge.

Look me in the eye with nothing less than complete human
compassion.
Tell me the Buddha-Fields, accordion-like, have opened—that we are
all awakened *in* one another and through.

A Certain Strain of Rain

I am a balcony of half-read scriptures.
I stood on a circle of ash and grew warm as the melting ice caps of Mars.

Nevertheless, I regret a cadence of tree fog swaying at me through the
  dark.
I regret a souvenir of Albuquerque rain, the slightest syllabic braid giving
  my tongue back part of its parched mouth.

What can I return to you now that I have brought the smelling salts?
What can you describe of leaving the body and bolstering the dark?

There is a vacancy of equal air, of independent saliva seeking the most
  inexact numeral.
When we momentarily depart, no one can tell if it is zero, one, or
  negative 553 into which we move.

There, blurred in the barbed-wire climb of hair, is a summer travel article
  on Kyoto and the spiritual swell of chrysanthemums.
It speaks of compassionate necessity, of tea ceremonies, even of flower
  arrangements arranging *us*.

For that reason the clocks kept cornering, having fierced a delirious if
  not altogether.
Yes, I truncate my speak. It's the only way I can get my tongue to remain
  constant. To disperse. To contain a certain—albeit absent—healing
  strain of rain.

We Stood Like Unfinished Kisses

He would describe the day's coverage as interest in French theatre, as
a lambaste, say—in the West—of Japanese Dada.
In the event of his own wrinkled elephant belly, the day could also
include fire-tinted leaves from the maternity halls of his stretch
marks.

Of course, some brought Tincture of Merthiolate.
Absolutely, it was the right thing to do.

A course of action resembles blood cupping the outer reaches of the
heart.
When, in the dream, they removed mine and replaced it with a third
kidney, I knew I was suddenly more cleanly alive.

We stood here and there like unfulfilled kisses.
Someone chanted seed-sounds. Taoist moaning from a T'ang tower.
And our entire sphere swayed from the weight of something *that*
beautiful.

I realized I had two tickets to view the Ubu plays performed in Fujian,
China.
There *is* no emperor when one readies himself, washes follicles of hair,
and contemplates the fragility of dead skin from four or five
incarnations back.

After so many lives, I heard a knocking and opened my door upon the
most beautiful face I had ever heard.
She said her name was *Bāgē—Starling—*but asked me to call her *Even
the Aching Rain*.

The Nearest and the Dearest

I could confide in fire only if my bones were real.
Sorrowfully, the elm tree holds the sun in hibernation under its winter
skin.

Similarly, I found a water clock inside the left vest pocket of every bride
from Bhutan.
I explicated the meaning of *timpani.* I spoke, *tamboura.* Revivified,
rarefied red.

Being born not quite alive also suggests space, at least its open scrawl in
the spine.
Strange drumming sounds from a deity deny mirrors the reflective
properties of words.

He wiped the axe, guided each cloak into a cutbank of snow.
I swear I saw the tree bark flinch, but now all he repeats is, *Mark my
scar.*

Who is he who eats the dog-nosed berry?
The already-here? The glue-my-mouth-quite-open?

Pheasant messages are transmitted by eating only the skin.
We get facials and magnify the year.

I once ate a monkfish and followed my star.
I recognized how near and far I already am.

Not to Dissolve *but* to Dissolve

But it is more than that, Promethean people stabbing at any
    mysterious sadness.
There is also great joy. We revolve our sleep breaths through one
    another to kiss the gooseflesh calm.

Said, *My manic mouth kept losing ink.*
Replied, *Some tender vowel sounds are good.*

Give me the fly-dung fix, the guinea fowl and her brown, brown egg.
It may be fertilized, but I will break my rule and eat it. Even here
    among the confused.

You are stunned? Baffled? Confounded, complete with qualms?
You are nonplussed, saddened in a sad way at my insistent dispersal of
    a shy voice?

When you examine a mirror, it will be there—in front of you—like the
    scar of sudden shoes.
Your feet are bare, the shoes too small, yet you keep trying to walk
    away.

When I entered the temple that full Ganges moon, the multiple-
    moaning ways of the body spasmed with fragments of lost internal
    song.
I will do everything in my power now not to dissolve *but* to dissolve
    into that truly grounded sound.

The Belt of Equatorial Calms

What can be said of the Belt of Equatorial Calms?
We still-mouth. We dropwort. We cry as the dead horse beats *us*.

We listless. We rain-ache. We whinge away the weeks.
This region of regions blows us further into whom and what we fear.

We say *yes* to nearly everything. Even the moon entering the vigorous
    canals of a shark's gills.
We restrain our tongues. Slap our own mouths. Take pains to invigorate
    our loss.

If the cosmogonic flea in the ear of the meditator.
If the doldrum winds and the lack of sea-salt hope.

If sitting and listening activates the cochlea of the inner ear. Nerve
    ganglia of the spine.
If we forever-and-again the language of leopard pace. If we learn how it
    sleeps roundly in a rainforest of sound.

Say we're finally calm enough to taste the dark spots thrown across our
    back.
Say we cross the great ocean of our day-to-day lies in a great good calm.

There are vulture blankets we use to blind and settle the fearful bird.
We cover ourselves in a darkness that removes us from flight. Learn the
    salt-craves of our bones as the salt-crave of all that is.

You Say I Fancy the Empty Drift

Nothing but your cheek and a pair of rubber gloves.
Nothing but a coping saw on the cockroach moss.

You say I fancy the empty drift, the equatorial tongue of both coasts at
   once.
You say, how ambiguous to hope for a channel of puzzled wind.

When the photographs arrived, I finally recognized my internal hurt.
Sure, I carry it well, I'm told, but bone silence is just that.

The only two birds without hollow bones are ostriches and penguins.
Actually, that's not true—much like I am confused in the latitudes of a
   funerary North.

How marvelous to realize we are the Hindu equivalent of the Holy
   Ghost.
In the City of Nine Gates, the darkness of the dictionaries proclaims us
   stable, transitive, and etymologically whole.

Body Rites

Because myth is the timbre of measure, let me utter the function of
    impediment.
I indicated an esoteric strain in my geographic representation, but you
    chose the demotic ravagings of my tongue.

There was a small labor camp we had all worked in.
It was called *A Theory of Discourse*.

The major problem is the euphoric cluster of grapes in sunlight by the
    window in the corner.
I am completed only in my unabridgement.

An apparent paradox might convey textures of the tongue.
My grandfather was chimney smoke. My grandmother, elm-bark
    kindling.

Lineaments of the earth's curves. Lineage of parallel bones plaguing me
    frown to frown.
When I moved next door, the nominative inscription of my past was
    performed with eel ash across my forehead. In the body rites of the
    swollen, suggestive dead.

Every Word You Fail

A radio dictation of prophetic contemplation is more than mere words.
Wash the sponge on the kitchen sink and feel starlings pass through
   the sole of your left foot.

I can't bear the thought that I might one day die.
More precisely, I can't bear the certainty in the word *might*.

Turning sixty-five should be easier.
I remember my father, so adult—younger then than I am now—left leg
   crossed over his right, as he expounded the importance of an
   education he never had.

That was the season of sepia, of Coca-Cola from tiny bottles burning
   the throat's back, of Mickey Mantle's broken leg and Kennedy's
   brain.
That was the time when middle-aged people *looked* old. When we
   cleaned the stone barbeque pit of mulberry stains and bird-blotch,
   believing something solid in coils of a pale green hose from
   Bennett's Hardware.

As I may have intended when choosing this body, there is a vortex of
   lifetimes of accumulated energy to which I comply.
Say my name backwards and poke it with a stick as it emerges in fits in
   sawdust droppings of a raccoon. In the scrawmings of cuttlefish.

I promise you this: the proceeds from this life will all be donated to the
   poor.
Bury my heart in India. The viscera and chest cavity beneath a rock
   cairn in Colorado.

Place the saliva from my mouth in a glass tube beneath a shagbark
   hickory in Indiana.
Scatter the ash and ask my tongue across every word you fail to speak.

The Distance Between the Coccyx and the Sacral

It was not in the script: a woman playing checkers alone on a tree
   stump, touching the board only when wind lifted the cottonwood
   leaves across the field.
I measured her feet from afar and knew she must have been
   purchasing illegal pigeons.

A bird begins to emerge whenever we reveal our multiple births.
I do not confide in the uninitiated. Their ears, as yet, are clogged with
   gnats.

Emerge. A bird emerges whenever we reveal the starling-severed
   hand.
One photographic granule of the Belgian Congo is enough to get me to
   clench every time I hear the words *elephant tusk* or *copper my
   mouth from Katanga*.

Then there was that previous life when we traded beads, dividing them
   equally, even among the dogs.
Still, someone always felt cheated, as if the other's bedding contained
   somehow-softer straw.

The time between incarnations is a sad glance.
The bones of the head vibrate and are silent.

Hand me the harmonica around the hobo fire.
Inscribe me my mouth.

The distance between the coccyx and the sacral can be immense.
Rain arrives as all rains do, fierce and full of mending.

Breathe in. Breathe out. Release the desire, even, for moon-fired owl
    flight.
There is a quiet like the long ending to a parade.

Notes

The epigraphs are drawn from Wang Wei, from "In My Lodge at Wang-Ch'uan After a Long Rain," translated by Witter Bynner from the texts of Kiang Kang-Hu, from *The Jade Mountain: A Chinese Anthology, Being Three Hundred Poems of the T'ang Dynasty, 618– 906*, Alfred A. Knopf, 1929 (Sixth Printing, 1945), and from Robert Desnos, from "Lying Down," translated by Carolyn Forché and William Kulik, from *The Selected Poems of Robert Desnos*, The Ecco Press, 1991.

"Unspecified Birth" is for Robert Kelly.

"6,000 Beards of Athos" takes its title from the book, *The 6,000 Beards of Athos*, by Ralph H. Brewster, Hogarth Press, 1935; reprint, Michael Russell (Publishing) Ltd, 1999.

In "Term," the phrases, "There are so many karmic seeds to expunge, this time, in the cool fires of the brain" and "altar of the spine," reference an advanced yogic meditation technique, often referred to by Paramahansa Yogananda as "roasting" karmic seeds "in the cool fires of the brain." Paramahansa Yogananda, *Autobiography of a Yogi*, Self-Realization Fellowship, 1946, Eighth Edition, 1959.

"Six Thousand Gold Pieces Buy the Lingering Death" and "Prefect Pai Talks and Laughs and Rights a Strange Injustice" take their titles from a chapter gloss in *The Travels of Lao Ts'an*, by Liu T'ieh-yun, translated by Harold Shadick, Columbia University Press, 1990.

"Lending You Your Scent" includes two phrases in stanza three and four (along with reference to César Vallejo), "The other one" and "That one," which echo repeated insistences from Vallejo's great poem, "The hungry man's wheel" [*sic*], from *The Complete Posthumous Poetry*, translated by Clayton Eshleman and José Rubia Barcia, University of California Press, 1978.

"Commands to Genii" draws its title from Wallace Stevens' notebooks of titles for poems that he collected but never used. Quoted in Nance Van Winckel, *The Writer's Chronicle,* March/April 2004.

"The Nearest and the Dearest" takes its title from a phrase in *The Upanishads: Breath of the Eternal*, translated by Swami Prabhavananda and Frederick Manchester. Copyright © 1948 by the Vedanta Society of Southern California, Vedanta Press (Mentor Books), 1964. The phrase "The nearest and the dearest" is often repeated by Paramahansa Yogananda, in lectures and books, to describe intimacy with the Divine Belovèd.

Part of the first line in "Body Rites" ("the function of impediment") alludes to the title of one of Marie Ponsot's books, *Admit Impediment*, Alfred A. Knopf, 1981. Ponsot's title itself references Shakespeare's "Sonnet 116": "Let me not to the marriage of true minds / Admit impediments," from *The Oxford Shakespeare: The Complete Sonnets and Poems*, Oxford University Press, Inc., 2002.

Selected Poetry Titles Published by SurVision Books

Seeds of Gravity: An Anthology of Contemporary Surrealist
Poetry from Ireland
Edited by Anatoly Kudryavitsky
ISBN 978-1-912963-18-8

Noelle Kocot. *Humanity*
(New Poetics: USA)
ISBN 978-1-9995903-0-7

Ciaran O'Driscoll. *The Speaking Trees*
(New Poetics: Ireland)
ISBN 978-1-9995903-1-4

Helen Ivory. *Maps of the Abandoned City*
(New Poetics: England)
ISBN 978-1-912963-04-1

John W. Sexton. *Inverted Night*
(New Poetics: Ireland)
ISBN 978-1-912963-05-8

Afric McGlinchey. *Invisible Insane*
(New Poetics: Ireland)
ISBN 978-1-9995903-3-8

Anatoly Kudryavitsky. *Stowaway*
(New Poetics: Ireland)
ISBN 978-1-9995903-2-1

Tim Murphy. *The Cacti Do Not Move*
(New Poetics: Ireland)
ISBN 978-1-912963-07-2

Clayre Benzadón. *Liminal Zenith*
(New Poetics: USA)
ISBN 978-1-912963-11-9

Thomas Townsley. *Tangent of Ardency*
(New Poetics: USA)
ISBN 978-1-912963-15-7

Matthew Geden. *Fruit*
(New Poetics: Ireland)
ISBN 978-1-912963-16-4

Marc Vincenz. *Einstein Fledermaus*
(New Poetics: USA)
ISBN 978-1-912963-20-1

Anton Yakovlev. *Chronos Dines Alone*
(Winner of James Tate Poetry Prize 2018)
ISBN 978-1-912963-01-0

Mikko Harvey & Jake Bauer. *Idaho Falls*
(Winner of James Tate Poetry Prize 2018)
ISBN 978-1-912963-02-7

Tony Bailie. *Mountain Under Heaven*
(Winner of James Tate Poetry Prize 2019)
ISBN 978-1-912963-09-6

Nicholas Alexander Hayes. *Amorphous Organics*
(Winner of James Tate Poetry Prize 2019)
ISBN 978-1-912963-10-2

John Bradley. *Spontaneous Mummification*
(Winner of James Tate Poetry Prize 2019)
ISBN 978-1-912963-13-3

John Thomas Allen. *Rolling in the Third Eye*
(Winner of James Tate Poetry Prize 2019)
ISBN 978-1-912963-15-7

Gary Glauber. *The Covalence of Equanimity*
(Winner of James Tate Poetry Prize 2019)
ISBN 978-1-912963-12-6

Charles Kell. *Pierre Mask*
(Winner of James Tate Poetry Prize 2019)
ISBN 978-1-912963-19-5

Alan Elyshevitz. *Mortal Hours*
(Winner of James Tate Poetry Prize 2020)
ISBN 978-1-912963-21-8

Henry Finch. *Reversing Falls*
(Winner of James Tate Poetry Prize 2020)
ISBN 978-1-912963-22-5

Jon Riccio. *Eye, Romanov*
(Winner of James Tate Poetry Prize 2020)
ISBN 978-1-912963-24-9

Alison Dunhill. *As Pure as Coal Dust*
(Winner of James Tate Poetry Prize 2020)
ISBN 978-1-912963-23-2

Thad DeVassie. *Splendid Irrationalities*
(Winner of James Tate Poetry Prize 2020)
ISBN 978-1-912963-25-6

George Kalamaras. *That Moment of Wept*
ISBN 978-1-9995903-7-6

Order our books from https://survisionmagazine.com/books.htm

www.ingramcontent.com/pod-product-compliance
Lightning Source LLC
LaVergne TN
LVHW021612080426
835510LV00019B/2529